S0-ASK-463

A Kid's Guide to Drawing™

How to Draw Cartoon Spacecraft and Astronauts in Action

Curt Visca and Kelley Visca

The Rosen Publishing Group's
PowerKids Press™
New York

Dedicated to our daughter, Kaytlin, who is out of this world!

Published in 2004 by The Rosen Publishing Group, Inc.
29 East 21st Street, New York, NY 10010

First Edition

Editor: Natashya Wilson

Book Design: Kim Sonsky

Layout Design: Michael J. Caroleo

Illustration Credits: All illustrations © Curt Visca.
Photo Credits: Cover and p. 6 courtesy of NASA/Charles M. Duke Jr.; p. 8 courtesy of NASA/Michael Collins; p. 10 courtesy of NASA/Harrison H. Schmitt; pp. 12, 14, 18 © Photodisc; pp. 16, 20 courtesy of NASA.

Visca, Curt.
How to draw cartoon spacecraft and astronauts in action / Curt Visca and Kelley Visca.
   p. cm. — (A kid's guide to drawing)
Summary: Provides facts about the space program, as well as step-by-step instructions for drawing cartoons of spacecraft and astronauts.
Includes bibliographical references and index.
ISBN 0-8239-6729-8 (library binding)
1. Space vehicles—Caricatures and cartoons—Juvenile literature. 2. Astronauts—Caricatures and cartoons—Juvenile literature. 3. Cartooning—Technique—Juvenile literature. [1. Cartooning—Technique. 2. Drawing—Technique.] I. Visca, Kelley. II. Title. III. Series.
NC1764.8.S72 V57 2004
741.5—dc21
                   2002011749

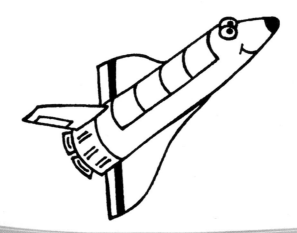

CONTENTS

1	Cartoon Spacecraft and Astronauts in Action	4
2	A Walk on the Moon	6
3	The Lunar Module	8
4	The Lunar Rover	10
5	The Space Shuttle	12
6	The Hubble Space Telescope	14
7	The *International Space Station*	16
8	Satellites	18
9	Rockets	20
	Terms for Drawing Cartoons	22
	Glossary	23
	Index	24
	Web Sites	24

Cartoon Spacecraft and Astronauts in Action

Many people dream about becoming **astronauts** and blasting off into outer space. "Astronaut" comes from the Latin words *astrum* and *nauta*, which mean "star" and "sailor." In 1961, Russian Yuri Gagarin became the first astronaut to travel in space. Nearly one month later, Alan Shepard became the first American to travel in space. Today about 400 astronauts from 20 countries have flown in space.

It is hard to become an astronaut. In the United States, more than 4,000 Americans apply for 20 astronaut positions every two years. Astronauts must have a college degree in engineering, math, or science. They must also have related work experience.

Astronauts train for one year. They learn about **astronomy**, **meteorology**, and other space-related subjects. They go through flight training and learn about **weightlessness**. On Earth, **gravity** keeps us on the ground. Gravity is not felt in space, so astronauts float! They train in machines called simulators, which make them feel as if they are floating in space.

In this book, you will see astronauts in action. You will learn about the spacecraft that send them into space, and about other objects in space. You will be able to draw a cartoon of each topic by following step-by-step drawings and directions. New steps are shown in red. The Terms for Drawing Cartoons list on page 22 can help you to do your cartoon drawings.

Cartoon drawings are different from **realistic** drawings. Realistic drawings look just like the objects being drawn. Cartoons are usually simpler drawings, made to be funny. You will add eyes, a nose, and a mouth to some of your cartoons. Real spacecraft don't have these **features**, but yours will!

You will need the following supplies to draw super spacecraft and astronauts in action:

- Paper
- A sharp pencil or a felt-tipped marker
- An eraser
- Colored pencils or crayons to add color

Collect your supplies, and draw your cartoons at a well-lit desk, a table, or another quiet place. Remember to take your time and to try your hardest. You'll be an all-star cartoonist in no time!

A Walk on the Moon

On July 20, 1969, Americans Edwin Aldrin and Neil Armstrong made history. They were the first people to set foot on the Moon. Armstrong said, "That's one small step for man, one giant leap for  mankind." Along with Michael Collins, they traveled to the Moon in the *Apollo 11* spacecraft. They arrived four days after **liftoff** from the Kennedy Space Center in Florida. Armstrong and Aldrin spent 21 ½ hours on the Moon. They collected rocks, took pictures, did experiments, and planted the American flag.

To walk on the Moon or to be outside in space, astronauts must wear special spacesuits. The suits protect their bodies from **temperatures** that range from 250°F to -250°F (151°C– -156°C). A control panel on the front works as a walkie-talkie so that the astronauts can talk to one another. A backpack filled with oxygen allows the astronauts to breathe.

1

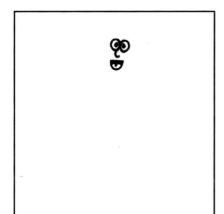

Start by making two circles with two dots inside for eyes. Draw a letter *C* for the nose. Make a straight line and a letter *U* for the mouth. Shade in the top of the mouth.

2

Outstanding! Draw a circle and a larger, slightly bent circle for the helmet. Make small letter *U*'s for hair. Draw curved lines for the ears. Add four short lines for the head.

3

Next draw two slightly bent lines for each arm. Add curved lines for the fingers.

4

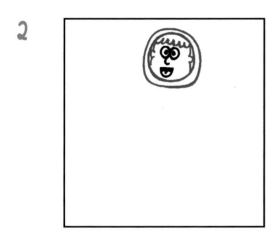

Draw slightly bent lines for the body and the outside of the legs. Make two bent lines for the inside of the legs. Draw a curved line and a wiggly line for each boot.

5

Make a rectangle on the chest for the control panel. Add two lines above it and below it. Draw two squares and four lines for the belt. Make four bent lines for the backpack.

6

Make wiggly lines to show the Moon. Draw detail, action lines, and a flag. Add stars and shading.

7

The Lunar Module

Apollo 11 was the first of six Apollo missions to put astronauts on the Moon. The **lunar module** is one of three parts of an Apollo spacecraft. It is the part that lands on the Moon. The service module carries food, air,

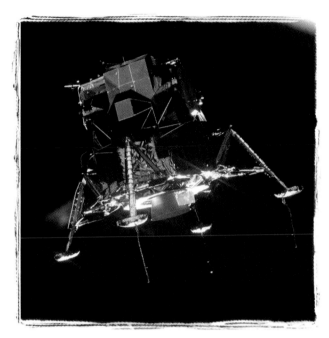

and other supplies. The command module is where the astronauts live. The lunar module stands nearly 23 feet (7 m) high and 31 feet (9.5 m) wide. The astronauts of the Apollo 11 mission named their lunar module the Eagle. When astronauts arrived at the Moon, the lunar module separated from the other modules and flew two astronauts down to the Moon. It had two parts. The lower part helped the module to land on the Moon. It carried equipment for exploring the Moon. Astronauts rode in the upper part. It had a place for the crew to work and a motor to take the astronauts back to the command module.

1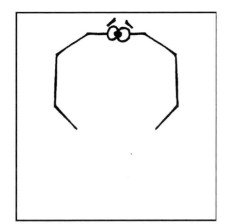

Draw two circles and two dots for eyes. Add two thick lines for eyebrows. Connect four straight lines on each side to make part of a stop-sign shape.

2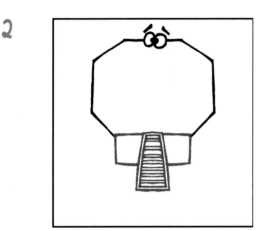

Make a slanted rectangle with another inside it. Draw many lines inside the rectangles. Draw four horizontal lines and two vertical lines for the bottom of the lunar module.

3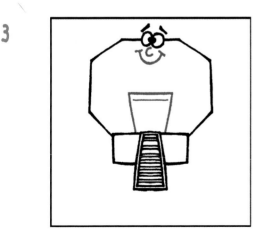

Incredible job! Make a letter C for the nose. Draw a letter U and two short lines for the mouth. Make two horizontal lines and two angled lines for the door.

4

Make two bent lines for each front leg. Draw two angled lines for each back leg. Make four oval shapes and four curved lines for the landing pads.

5

Sensational work! Next make two rectangles and three triangles on each side for panel instruments. Draw two straight lines for each arm and five curved lines for each hand.

6

Add detail on the module. Draw wiggly lines and dots for the Moon. Add stars and shading.

9

The Lunar Rover

The lunar rover is a special type of car that was used by astronauts on the *Apollo 15, 16,* and *17* missions to travel across the Moon's rocky surface. It is also called a moon buggy. The lunar rover is more than 10 feet (3 m) long and 6 feet (2 m) wide. It is battery powered and can reach a top speed of 9 miles per hour (14 km/h). The lunar rover does not have a roof. It has two seats that look like lawn chairs. Each lunar rover has an umbrella-shaped **antenna** and a TV camera on its front. The lunar rover can carry one or two astronauts, equipment, and rock samples collected by the astronauts. Astronauts have collected more than 800 pounds (363 kg) of moon rocks and soil. When astronauts were not using the lunar rover, they folded it up and stored it in the lunar module.

1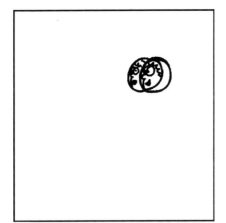

Make a circle and a curved line for the right helmet. Draw a letter *C* for the left helmet. Add circles and dots for eyes. Make noses and mouths. Draw lines for cheeks, and add hair.

2

Make bent lines for the arms, legs, bodies, and boots. Make letter *U*'s for fingers. Make curved and straight lines for the control stick. Add bent lines for the backpack and the seat.

3

Make a foot pedal. Draw two curved lines and two short lines for each fender. Add four circles and wiggly lines for the wheels. Make the bottom using straight lines and rectangles.

4

Next draw rectangles, squares, and straight lines for the front and back parts of the lunar rover. Make a straight line with a dot on top for one antenna. Use a triangle for another.

5

For the big antenna, start with two vertical lines and a square. Add a wide letter *U* and three big wiggly lines. Add two more vertical lines and an oval at the top.

6

Draw detail on your rover. Add wiggly lines for the Moon. Add more detail, stars, and shading.

11

The Space Shuttle

The space shuttle is the world's first **reusable** spacecraft. It is **launched** into space on a rocket, and it lands like an airplane. The first space shuttle to fly into space was the *Columbia*, in 1981. Five different space shuttles have flown on a total of more than 110 missions. More than 600 astronauts have flown on space shuttle missions. Space shuttles have sent more than 3 million pounds (1.4 million kg) of **cargo** into **orbit**. A space shuttle is made up of three parts. The **orbiter** has a cabin that can carry eight crew members. It can also carry satellites, spacecraft, and scientific laboratories, such as *Skylab*, in its **payload bay**. The second part is a large tank that carries fuel for the main engines. The third part has two **rocket boosters**. They provide extra power during the first 2 minutes after liftoff.

1

Begin by drawing a circle, a curved line, and two dots for eyes. Make a rounded, sideways letter V with a line at the end for the front. Shade in the tip.

2

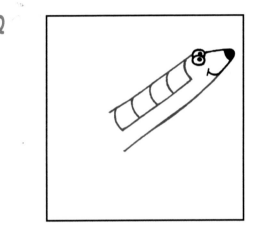

Next make two long lines for the body. Draw a straight line down the middle of the body, then add five curved lines to show the payload bay.

3

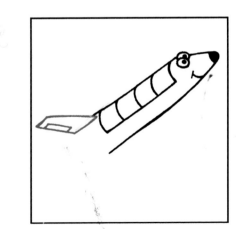

Perfect! Next make three straight lines and one bent line for the tail fin. Add a small rectangle inside for detail.

4

Draw two curved lines and a straight line at the end of the body. Add lines inside for detail. Draw two straight lines and two curved lines to make each rocket engine.

5

You did it! Next make a straight line and a curved line for each wing. Draw a thick line on each wing for detail.

6

Add a flag and "USA" on your space shuttle. Draw action lines. Add stars, smoke, and shading.

The Hubble Space Telescope

The Hubble Space Telescope has made it possible for people to see space better than ever before. The Hubble was launched in 1990. At 43 ½ feet (13 m) long and 14 feet (4 m) wide, it is the largest telescope in space. The

Hubble uses mirrors to show objects in space. Its main mirror is 8 feet (2.5 m) wide. There are two large, flat **solar** panels on either side of the telescope. They change sunlight into electricity. The Hubble sends pictures and facts to Earth using radio waves. It has helped scientists to measure the distances of stars from Earth, to learn more about the air around Jupiter, and to find new **galaxies**. Scientists now know of 125 billion galaxies! The Hubble has traveled almost 1.5 billion miles (2.5 billion km). It circles Earth once every 100 minutes, traveling at 17,000 miles per hour (27,359 km/h), 375 miles (603.5 km) above Earth.

1

Draw two ovals and put a dot inside each one for the eyes.

2

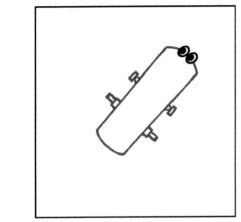

Draw a slightly curved line by each eye. Add two long straight lines and another curved line for the body of your Hubble telescope. Add squares and rectangles on each side.

3

Wow! Next make a letter C for the nose. Draw a letter U with one straight line on each end for the mouth.

4

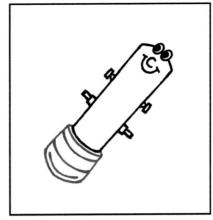

I'm proud of you! Start the bottom of your Hubble using two short angled lines. Add three curved rectangle shapes. Draw a curved line in the bottom unit for detail.

5

For each solar panel, first make a long rectangle. Add two straight lines across its middle. Draw a lot of small rectangles on either side of the lines.

6

Add detail, action lines, and an astronaut. Write "USA."
Draw a curved line and dots for Earth. Add stars and shading.

The International Space Station

The *International Space Station* (*ISS*) is a spacecraft in which astronauts can live for months at a time. The first part of the *ISS*  was launched in November 1998. It orbits Earth once every 90 minutes. Once the *ISS* is finished, in about 2006, it will be the world's largest spacecraft. It will measure 356-by-290 feet (108.5-by-88.5 m) and will weigh 496 tons (450 t). Many countries are helping to build the *ISS*, including the United States, Canada, Russia, Japan, and Brazil. When it is finished, the *ISS* will have six **laboratories** for science experiments. Crews of up to seven astronauts from around the world will do experiments, build and repair spacecraft, and train other astronauts. Experiments are being done now in the *ISS* to study the effect that weightlessness has on the human body.

1

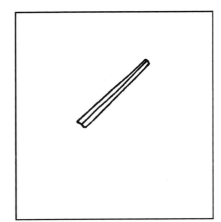

The picture on the left shows the *ISS* as it looked in 2002. We're going to draw it as it will look when it's done! Begin by making a long rectangle with a line in the center.

2

Next draw three small squares and a curved line at one end of the rectangle. Draw a rectangle with three lines inside for each solar panel. Use circles to attach the panels.

3

Repeat step 2 on the other end. Make the solar panels larger on this side so that they look closer!

4

Make two sets of five curved lines above the first rectangle. Draw letter *U*'s below them. Add three thin oval shapes. Attach two more solar panels to the top of the longest oval.

5

That was a tough step! Next draw the front of the *ISS* using circles, curved lines, and straight lines. Make two lines of small squares under the solar panels on the right.

6

Draw a cartoon Earth to show that your *ISS* is in space! Add action lines, stars, and shading.

17

Satellites

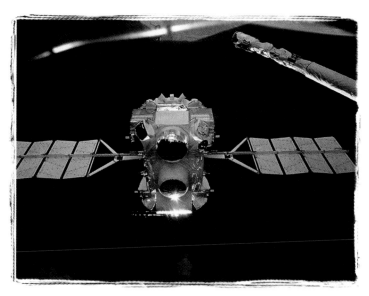

Satellites are objects that orbit other objects in space. On October 4, 1957, the Soviet Union launched the first humanmade satellite, *Sputnik*, into space to orbit Earth. *Sputnik 2* was sent into space a month later, with a dog named Laika inside as a passenger. Laika was the first space traveler!

There are many different types of humanmade satellites. **Communications** satellites carry radio, television, and telephone signals around the world. **Navigational** satellites, also called global positioning satellites, help people such as sailors and airplane pilots to know where they are on Earth. Weather satellites help **meteorologists** to track the weather. U.S. military satellites take pictures of different countries to use to keep the United States safe. Scientific satellites study Earth, the stars, and other planets. More than 2,500 satellites are currently orbiting Earth.

1

Let's draw a communications satellite. Start by drawing two circles and two dots for the eyes. Make a square around the eyes.

2

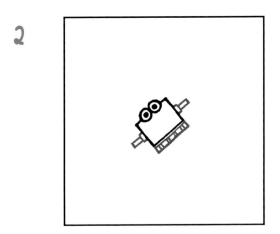

Add two long rectangles and four pairs of short straight lines at the bottom. Draw two small rectangles on each side.

3

Wonderful! Next make a letter *U* for the nose. Draw a bigger letter *U* and two short lines for the mouth.

4

Keep smiling! For each solar panel, make a large rectangle with 15 smaller rectangles inside.

5

Draw the Moon! Make an oval, a curved line, and two dots for the eyes. Add another curved line for the nose. Make two curved lines and a big letter *C* for the Moon's shape. Add a letter *U* and a short line for the mouth.

6

Draw a curved line, dots, and wiggly lines for Earth. Add action lines, stars, and shading. Super job!

19

Rockets

Rockets power themselves by burning fuel and pushing out the **exhaust** the burning fuel makes. Many rockets look like tubes with cone-shaped tops. Some are used to launch spacecraft. These rockets are very powerful. They reach speeds of 25,000 miles per hour (40,234 km/h). They are made up of several smaller rockets, called stages. The first stage has rockets called boosters attached to it to add more power for liftoff. The second stage makes the rocket go faster. The third stage puts it into orbit. Once the fuel in a stage is used up, the stage drops off and usually burns up in Earth's **atmosphere**. Some stages can be used again, such as the rocket boosters on the space shuttle. Saturn V rockets are the most powerful. They were used to launch the *Apollo* spacecraft. With the *Apollo* spacecraft attached, the Saturn V measured about 364 feet (111 m) in length and weighed about 6 million pounds (3 million kg).

1

Let's create our last drawing! Make two circles and two dots for the eyes. Draw an upside-down letter *V* for the cone-shaped top of your rocket.

2

Make two vertical lines for the side of your rocket. Draw a letter *C* for the nose. Make a straight line and a letter *U* for the mouth. Shade it in.

3

Great work! Next make two angled lines and two long vertical lines. Add four thick horizontal lines.

4

Make two triangles on the bottom for the rocket's nozzles, which let out the exhaust. Add a thick line for the launch pad. I'm proud of you!

5

Start the launch tower with a long rectangle. Add smaller rectangles and straight lines for tower platforms. Make a smoke cloud from curved lines.

6

Write "USA" and draw a flag on your rocket. Add birds, clouds, and shading. Blast off!

21

Terms for Drawing Cartoons

Here are some of the words and shapes that you will use to draw cartoon spacecraft and astronauts in action:

⸌⸍	Action lines	V	Letter V
⫽	Angled lines	⬭	Oval
𝄇	Bent lines	▭	Rectangle
◯	Circle	⬛	Shading
⌒	Curved line	☐	Square
Ɛ∷ᵛᵛ	Detail	★	Star
∴∵	Dots	☰	Straight lines
—	Horizontal line	▬	Thick line
C	Letter C	|	Vertical line
U	Letter U	∿	Wiggly lines

Glossary

antenna (an-TEH-nuh) A metal object used to send and receive signals.

astronauts (AS-troh-nots) People who are trained to travel in outer space.

astronomy (uh-STRAH-nuh-mee) The science of the Sun, the Moon, planets, and stars.

atmosphere (AT-muh-sfeer) The layer of gases around an object in space. On Earth, this layer is air.

cargo (KAR-goh) The load of goods carried by a spacecraft.

communications (kuh-myoo-nih-KAY-shunz) The sharing of facts or feelings.

exhaust (ig-ZOST) Smoky air made by burning gas or other fuels.

features (FEE-churz) The special look or form of a person or an object.

galaxies (GA-lik-seez) Large groups of stars and the planets that circle them.

gravity (GRA-vih-tee) The natural force that causes objects to move toward the center of Earth.

laboratories (LA-bruh-tor-eez) Rooms in which scientists do tests.

launched (LONCHD) Pushed out or put into the air.

liftoff (LIFT-of) An upward takeoff by a rocket or an aircraft.

lunar (LOO-ner) Of or about the Moon.

meteorologists (mee-tee-uh-RAH-luh-jists) People who study the weather.

meteorology (mee-tee-uh-RAH-luh-jee) The study of the weather.

module (MAH-jul) A unit or a part.

navigational (nah-vuh-GAY-shuh-nul) Having to do with finding out which way ships and other moving things are headed.

orbit (OR-bit) A circular path.

orbiter (OR-bih-ter) The part of a space shuttle that carries the crew.

payload bay (PAY-lohd BAY) The trunk of a space shuttle, in which necessary items are kept.

realistic (ree-uh-LIS-tik) Made to look real or true to life.

reusable (ree-YOO-zuh-bul) Able to be used again.

rocket boosters (RAH-kit BOO-sterz) Engines attached to a spacecraft to add power.

satellites (SA-til-yts) Spacecraft that circle Earth.

solar (SOH-ler) Powered by energy from the Sun.

temperatures (TEM-pruh-churz) How hot or cold things are.

weightlessness (WAYT-les-nes) Feeling no downward pull.

23

Index

A
Aldrin, Edwin, 6
Apollo 11, 6, 8
Armstrong, Neil, 6

C
Collins, Michael, 6
Columbia, 12
command module, 8

E
Eagle, 8

G
Gagarin, Yuri, 4
galaxies, 14

H
Hubble Space
    Telescope, 14

I
*International Space
    Station (ISS)*, 16

K
Kennedy Space
    Center, 6

L
laboratories, 16
Laika, 18
lunar module, 8, 10
lunar rover, 10

M
meteorologists, 18
Moon, 6, 8, 10

R
rocket boosters, 12,
    20

S
satellites, 18
Saturn V, 20
service module, 8
Shepard, Alan, 4
simulators, 4
Skylab, 12
solar panels, 14
space shuttle, 12
spacesuits, 6
Sputnik, 18
Sputnik 2, 18

Web Sites

Due to the changing nature of Internet links, PowerKids Press has developed an online list of Web sites related to the subject of this book. This site is updated regularly. Please use this link to access the list: www.powerkidslinks.com/kgd/spacecra/